Not Just a Game

**Brandon Robshaw
and
Rochelle Scholar**

Published in association with
The Basic Skills Agency

Hodder & Stoughton

A MEMBER OF THE HODDER HEADLINE GROUP

Acknowledgements
Illustrations: Chris Rothero / Linden Artists.
Cover: Shane Marsh / Linden Artists.

Orders: please contact Bookpoint Ltd, 39 Milton Park, Abingdon, Oxon OX14
4TD. Telephone: (44) 01235 400414, Fax: (44) 01235 400454. Lines are open
from 9.00–6.00, Monday to Saturday, with a 24 hour message answering
service. Email address: orders@bookpoint.co.uk

British Library Cataloguing in Publication Data
A catalogue record for this title is available from The British Library

ISBN 0 340 72103 0

First published 1998
Impression number   10 9 8 7 6 5 4 3 2
Year   2003 2002 2001 2000 1999 1998

Typeset by Fakenham Photosetting Ltd, Fakenham, Norfolk.
Printed in Great Britain for Hodder & Stoughton Educational, a division of
Hodder Headline Plc, 338 Euston Road, London NW1 3BH by Athenaeum
Press Ltd, Gateshead, Tyne & Wear.

About the play

The People

- **Josh**
- **Steve**
- **Hassan**
- **Coach**

The Place

Buston Rovers Football Club.

What's Happening

Josh, *Steve* and *Hassan* are
waiting outside the
Coach's *office.*

Act 1

Josh	Why do you think he wants to see us?
Steve	To tell us how good we are!
Hassan	I don't think so. We got beat 3–0 on Saturday by Southampton Reserves.
Josh	Yeah, but that wasn't our fault.
Steve	That's right. It was the others who played badly. We played all right.
Josh	We're the three best players he's got.
Steve	And I'm the best of the lot!
Josh	Who says?
Hassan	His mum!

Steve	No, not just my mum.
	My dad thinks so too.
Josh	The point is, us three
	are his star players.
	I bet he wants to sign us.
Hassan	Sign us?
Josh	Yeah. Sign us up for Rovers.
	As professionals.
Hassan	Professionals?
	Do you really think so?
Steve	Wouldn't that be great?
	No more cleaning the boots
	for the first team.
Josh	No more trying to live
	on fifty quid a week.
Steve	We'll be rich.
Josh	Rolling in it.

Hassan	I'm going to buy a great big house with a swimming pool.
Josh	I'm going to buy a BMW.
Steve	We'll be on the telly. On Match of the Day.
Josh	We'll be famous. All the girls will fancy us.

Steve	I'm going to go out with a Spice Girl.
Josh	So am I.
Hassan	How many Spice Girls are there?
Josh	There's five. But one's going out with David Beckham.
Steve	That leaves four. Enough for one each – and one left over!
Hassan	We'll all go out with a Spice Girl!
Steve	I'm going to go out with two!

The office door opens.
*The **Coach** is standing there.*

Coach	OK, lads, come in. I want to talk to you.

Act 2

*In the **Coach**'s office.*

Coach   Right. You've all been here nearly
two years on YTS,
haven't you?

Josh   Yeah. It will be two years
next Saturday, boss.

Coach   And before that, you did two years
at the Centre of Excellence.
That's four years of training.
And it's nearly over.

Hassan   So ... what happens next?

Coach   What happens next?
Good question.
Are you ready to be professionals?

Hassan	Yes!
Steve	Yes!
Josh	Yes!
Coach	I'm not so sure.
	I don't think you are.
Steve	What?
Hassan	Why not?
Josh	I thought we were
	the star players!
Coach	It's easy to be a star player
	in the reserves, playing with
	a bunch of other teenagers.
	It takes something special
	to be a professional.
	Have you got what it takes?
Steve	Well, I have.
Josh	So have I.
Hassan	Me too.

Coach	That's what you think, is it?
Josh	Yeah.
Steve	That's what we think.
Coach	Now let me tell you what I think.
	Steve – you're tall and you head
	the ball well.
	You've got a good shot.
	You've scored a lot of goals
	for the reserves this season.
	You're a good attacking player.

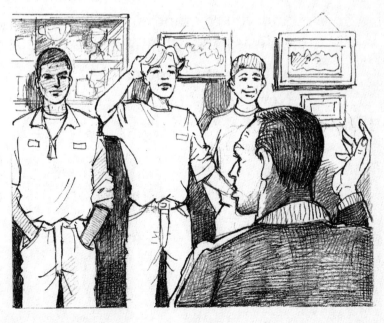

Steve	So what's the problem?
Coach	The problem is, you're not
	a team player. You're selfish.
	You don't help the others.
	Last Saturday, when we were 3–0
	down against Southampton,
	what were you doing?
Steve	I was trying to score, wasn't I?
Coach	You were standing about
	up front waiting for the ball
	to come to you.
	Everyone else is back defending
	and you're standing about
	up front like a blind date
	at the wrong cinema.
	Now, Josh ...
Josh	Yes boss?

Coach	You're not a selfish player.
	You pass the ball well. Very well.
	A lot of Steve's goals
	this season are thanks to you.
	And you've got good pace. But ...
Josh	But what?
Coach	You only play well
	when things are going well.
	When we're losing, you lose heart.
	You get lazy.
	In that Southampton game,
	in the second half
	you lost all your pace.
	Players not as quick as you
	were beating you to the ball.
	Now, Hassan, he never stops
	trying.
Hassan	Oh. Thanks boss!

Coach	You've also got brilliant control.
	I've never seen a player
	your age with better control.
	But …
Hassan	What? What's wrong?
Coach	You can control the ball,
	but you can't control your temper.
	And when you get angry,
	you're all over the place.
	That Southampton forward had
	a go at you on Saturday, didn't he?
Hassan	Yes. He did.
Coach	And after that, you were
	all over the place.
	Trying to beat everyone
	on your own.
	Giving the ball away.
	Making bad tackles.
	You were lucky not to get sent off
	when you brought him down.

Hassan	He's lucky I didn't break his legs.
	Racist prat.
Coach	Called you a Paki, did he?
Hassan	Yes. And other things.
Coach	I'm sorry, Hassan. It's not nice.
	But not all footballers are nice.
	If you can't take it …
Hassan	Why should I have to take it?
Coach	If you were a professional,
	you'd have to take it.
	There aren't many Asian
	professionals
	and you'd get a lot of stick.
	If you can't play at your best
	when the going gets tough,
	you won't make it.
Steve	He's right, Hassan.

Coach	That goes for all of you!
	You've got to play at your best
	when things get tough.
	If you can't do that,
	you'll never be professionals.
Josh	So – what are you saying?
	You're not going to sign us up?
Steve	Four years – wasted!
Coach	Wait a minute.
	I haven't made up my mind yet.
	There's one more game to go.
Josh	Against Man United reserves.
Coach	And that will be a tough game.
	If you can play at your best
	and show me how much
	you want it – I'll sign you.
Steve	What – all of us?

Coach	If you all play well. Or maybe I'll sign just two of you. Or one of you. Or none of you. It's up to you. It depends how much you want it.
Hassan	Oh, I want it all right.
Josh	So do I!
Steve	Me too! I want it the most!
Coach	We'll see who wants it the most on Saturday.

Act 3

In the dressing room,
before the match on Saturday.

Josh   This is it, then.

Steve   The big one.

Josh   Are you nervous?

Steve   What, me? Nervous?

Josh   Yeah, you. Nervous.

Steve   You must be joking.

             Of course I'm not nervous.

Josh   Why are you shaking, then?

Steve   I'm not shaking.

             I'm just – loosening up.

Hassan   Well, I'm nervous. I'm terrified.

Josh   So am I!

Steve	Oh, all right, then –
	I am a bit nervous.
	That's why I brought my mascot.
	See?
Hassan	What is it?
Steve	It's a lucky rabbit's foot.
Hassan	Wasn't so lucky for the rabbit,
	was it?
Josh	I've got a mascot too.
	A little teddy bear. I always used
	to take this into exams at school.
Hassan	Did it work?
Josh	No, I failed the lot of them.
Steve	Have you got a mascot, Hass?
Hassan	I'm wearing my favourite pants.
Josh	Favourite pants!
Steve	Favourite pants won't be
	much use against Man United.
Josh	No use at all.

Steve	They won't care what pants you're wearing.
Hassan	I know. It just makes me feel better to know I've got them on.

Pause

Josh	It's going to be hard.
Steve	We've got to remember what he said.
Hassan	Got to show how much we want it.
Steve	I've got to help the team more. Pass the ball more.
Hassan	I've got to keep cool when players have a go at me.
Josh	And I've got to keep playing really hard even when we're losing. Which we will be, against Man United.
Hassan	Yeah, they're a good side.

Steve   A hell of a good side.

Hassan   They've got players in the reserves who'd walk into our first team.

Steve   We've got to give 90% for 100 minutes.

Josh   No, it's the other way round.

Steve   What?

Josh   You mean 100% for 90 minutes.

Steve   Whatever.

Pause

17

Josh	What if they hammer us?
Hassan	What if they beat us 5–0?
	Or 6–0? Or 7–0? Or – ?
Steve	All right, all right, shut up.
	Let's calm down. It's just a game
	of football, right?
Hassan	No, it's not just a game!
	It's more than that! Much more!
	It's our future! It's the difference
	between having a career
	and having nothing!
Josh	He's right. Football is the only
	thing I'm any good at. If they
	don't sign me, what am I going
	to do?
Hassan	If we do well in this match,
	we'll be professionals.
	We'll get paid good money for
	doing something we love.

Josh	And if we don't do well,
	we'll be on the dole.
Steve	There's other clubs.
Hassan	But they won't want you if you
	say it's just a game.
	It's not just a game! Not to us.

Pause

Josh	I wonder how we'll be feeling
	in two hours time.
Steve	In two hours time, we'll know.

Act 4

In the dressing room, after the match.

Josh One all! I can't believe it!

Steve We drew! We drew with the mighty Man United!

Josh And I scored.

Steve I made that goal. I was the one who crossed the ball.

Josh I know. It was a good cross. Thanks.

Steve That's OK. You took it well.

Josh We could have beaten them.

Hassan We should have beaten them! We were the better team.

Steve We missed too many chances.

Hassan I know. I missed one.

Josh That's OK, Hass. You're a midfielder, not a striker.

Steve   You played fine in midfield, Hass.
Don't worry.

Hassan   I played all right, but – I wish
I'd scored that goal.
I wish we'd beaten them.

Josh   You played well. You kept your
cool when that Man United
forward asked you for a chicken
vindaloo with plain rice.

Hassan   Maybe I was too cool. Maybe I
could have played with more fire.
You two will get it. I won't.

Steve   No, no, you did fine.
You kept it tight in midfield.
And I put that cross in.
And Josh scored. All three of us
did well – he'll have to sign us all!

Josh	Thank God for your lucky rabbit's foot and my little teddy bear and Hassan's favourite pants!
Steve	We're going to be professionals!
Josh	Getting paid for doing something we love!
Steve	Driving BMWs!
Josh	Going out with Spice Girls.
Hassan	We'll see.

Act 5

*In the **Coach**'s office.*

Coach Right, lads. That was your
last game as YTS trainees.

Josh So? How did we do?

Coach How do you think you did?

Steve We did great.
We drew with Man United!

Josh You've got to say that's
a great result, haven't you?
To draw with Man United
Reserves.
I'm over the moon!

Coach Hassan?

Hassan We should have beaten them.

Coach You're not happy with a draw?

Hassan We could have won today
and we didn't. And it's my fault.

Steve	Oh, come on, Hass,
	it wasn't your fault.
Hassan	I missed that goal, didn't I?
Josh	It wasn't such an easy chance.
Hassan	If I'd scored, we'd have won.
Steve	Yeah, but a draw's
	not so bad, is it?
	Not against Man United.
Josh	A draw's a great result
	against a team like Man United.
Coach	All right. I've made up my mind.
Steve	Have you? Are you signing me?
Josh	Are you signing me?
Coach	I'm signing you, Hassan.
	I'm sorry, Steve. Sorry, Josh.
	I won't be able to sign you two.
Josh	What? You must be joking!
Steve	What? Hassan missed a chance!
Coach	I know. But Hassan had
	a good game apart from that.
	He kept his cool. And he kept
	possession for us in midfield.

Josh	Yeah, but I scored!
Steve	And I made that goal!
Coach	I know. You all played well today. The fact is, you've all got talent. But Hassan has got something more.
Steve	What?
Coach	He's got the attitude. He wants to win. He wants to win so much he's not happy with a draw. Even against Man United Reserves. A draw's good enough for you two. But it's not good enough for Hassan. *(He steps forward and shakes **Hassan**'s hand)* Welcome to Buston Rovers, Hassan.

Epilogue

Hassan became a regular First Team player
for Buston Rovers and had a long and successful
career in the Premier Division.
He was capped twenty-one times
as an England international.

Josh ended up by being signed
as a professional for Leyton Orient.
He made a living out of the game
but never played in the Premier Division.

Steve gave up trying
to become a professional.
He now runs a hardware store.
He still plays football on Sundays
for a local amateur club.